ORANGUTAN

by CAROLINE ARNOLD

Photographs by RICHARD HEWETT

MORROW JUNIOR BOOKS · NEW YORK

Library of Congress Cataloging-in-Publication Data. Arnold, Caroline. Orangutan/by Caroline Arnold; photographs by Richard Hewett. p.   cm. Summary: Depicts the physical characteristics and behavior of the orangutan and discusses the possible future of the species. ISBN 0-688-08826-0.—ISBN 0-688-08827-9 (lib. bdg.)
1. Orangutan—Juvenile literature. [1. Orangutan.] I. Hewett, Richard, ill. II. Title.
QL737.P96A76 1990 599.88′42—dc20 89-38957 CIP AC

Acknowledgments

This book could not have been written without the assistance of the Los Angeles Zoo, and we want to thank everyone there who helped us. In particular, we want to express our appreciation to June Bottcher, for helping to make all the necessary arrangements, and to Don Richardson, the orang keeper. We also thank our editor, Andrea Curley, for her continued enthusiastic support.

Like many other zoos, the Los Angeles Zoo allows people to donate money and "adopt" one of the zoo animals through their Adopt an Animal program. The adopted animal does not actually belong to the donor. It lives at the zoo and is cared for by zookeepers. However, the donor receives a certificate and can choose a name for the animal. All of the orangs have been adopted except for Louis, who is on loan from the San Diego Zoo.

The orangs also have names given to them by the keepers and we have used those names in the book. The following are the orangutans, their zoo names first and their adopted names in parentheses: Willie (Cahalas), Louie (Puff), Michael (Bingham), Pumpkin (Milken), Sally (Flakkee Sleepy Time), Eloise (Maxine), Ember (Adriane), Rosie (Rosie), and Kalim (Peanuts).

THE sun was just rising over the hillside as the orangutans came out into the fresh morning air. Using all four limbs, Sally, one of the large orangs, climbed nimbly over a large rock. On her back, young Michael clung tightly to her long hair as he peered ahead. He was curious to find out what the keeper had left for them to eat and play with.

When the orangutans got to the open area on the other side of the enclosure, they discovered a large pile of leafy green stalks. Michael scrambled down off Sally's back, and while she and the other orangs greeted each other, the little orang grabbed a small stalk and sat down to chew it.

One-and-a-half-year-old Michael is the youngest member of a group of ten orangutans that lives at the Los Angeles Zoo in California. Like most of the other orangs, Michael had been born at the zoo and named by the keepers. The orangutans learn to recognize their names and respond to them when they are spoken to. In addition to Michael and Sally, the group includes two adult males, Louis and Willie; Sally's grown daughter Eloise; four adolescents, Louie, Ember, Rosie, and Kalim; and another youngster named Pumpkin. Because individual orangs vary in size, appearance, and personality, the keepers have no trouble telling them apart.

The orangutans at the zoo live in a large outdoor area that allows them to move about freely and to interact with each other. It consists of a large island surrounded by a deep moat and steep walls. On the island is a small pond, rocks for shade and resting places, and a network of ropes and logs for climbing. At the back, a passage leads to an inside room where the orangs stay at night and when it is cold or rainy. Although the climate in Southern California is less humid and cooler than that of the tropical forests where wild orangutans live, the zoo orangs are comfortable and can be outdoors all year.

Orangutans are gentle and do not ordinarily attack people or other animals, although they will defend themselves if they feel threatened. The keepers at the zoo know the orangutans well, but they are always careful around them and do not go into their enclosure when the animals are in it. The keepers clean the outside area each morning while the orangutans are still indoors; then, during the day, they clean their inside quarters.

In ancient times orangutans lived throughout the southeast Asia area. Today, however, wild orangutans are found only on the islands of Borneo and Sumatra, where they live in dense tropical rain forests. The orangs depend on the trees in the forest for food, for shelter, and as protection from dangers below. Unfortunately many of the trees have been cut down for fuel and lumber, and to clear land for farming. When the trees disappear, the orangs have nowhere to live. Without care and protection, these magnificent apes are in great danger of becoming extinct.

In an effort to save orangutans, people are trying to learn more about them before it is too late. Scientists are studying orangutans in their natural environment as well as in zoos and research centers. As with all wild animals living outside their natural environment, the behavior of orangutans changes somewhat as they adapt to captivity. Nevertheless, everything that we can learn about these animals helps to promote their survival.

One of the most remarkable things about orangutans is how similar they are to people, both in body structure and in some of the ways they behave. Along with gorillas and chimpanzees, orangutans are more closely related to human beings than any other animal. Scientists believe that we have all evolved from an apelike creature that lived about 10 million years ago. During the course of evolution, many changes took place that made humans distinct from these animals. Yet by studying how the apes have adapted to the environments in which they live, we can learn about the origins of some of our own behaviors and gain insights into our natural heritage.

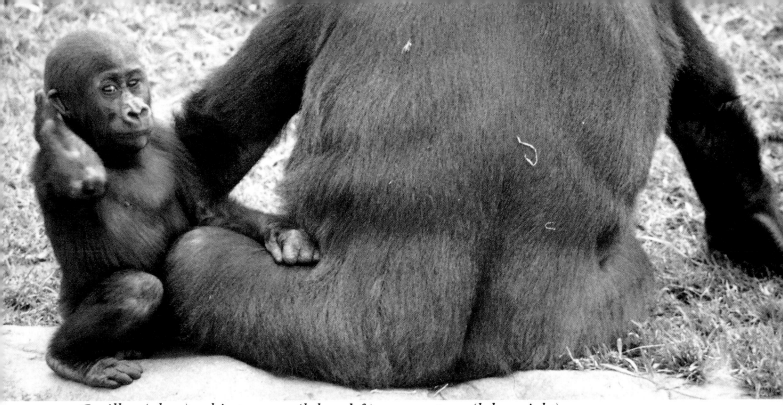

Gorillas (above), chimpanzees (below left), orangutans (below right).

Apes are divided into two groups: the great apes, which are the orangutans, gorillas, and chimpanzees; and the lesser apes, which include seven species of gibbons. Gorillas and chimpanzees live in Africa, whereas orangutans and gibbons live in the vicinity of southeast Asia. The lesser apes are acrobatic tree-dwelling animals, and are believed to have evolved earlier than the larger great apes. Unlike most monkeys, apes do not have tails. All apes belong to the family group called the pongids.

The gorilla is the largest of the great apes, with males that can reach 450 pounds (204.5 kilograms) or more. The gorilla lives mainly on the ground and is a heavy, stocky animal. Chimpanzees, the smallest of the great apes, live both on the ground and in the lower branches of trees. They are considered to be the most closely related to humans because they share more of the same body chemicals. Compared to the chimpanzee and gorilla, the orangutan has a more elongated shape, with a lighter weight in relation to its height. This suits its life in the forest, where long arms and a more agile shape make moving through the treetops easier.

Gibbon

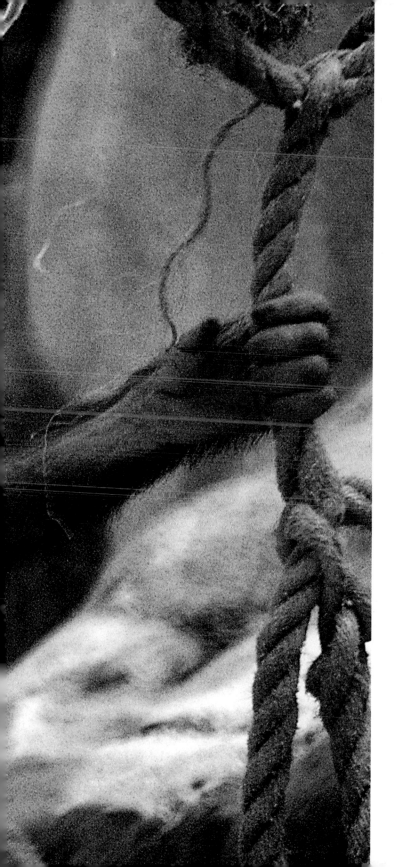

Apes and people are part of a larger animal group called primates. Other primates include monkeys, marmosets, and shrews. The one common characteristic of all primates is the ability to climb by grasping. Some primates, like orangutans, can climb using both their hands and feet. Their toes are long and flexible, which allows them to hold and manipulate objects as well.

An orangutan's hand is larger than a human hand, and the fingers are much longer in proportion to the thumb. This helps the orang to hold on tightly when climbing. When an orang hangs onto a branch or vine, the top joint of the fingers can wrap around the branch completely to form a locking grip. This grip is so strong that an orang can easily support its entire body weight with one hand.

Orangutans are noted for their unbelievable strength and have well-developed arm and shoulder muscles. In their native lands, they are said to be powerful enough to kill crocodiles with their bare hands.

Willie, a male Sumatran orangutan.

The name "orangutan" is formed from two Malay words, *orang* and *hutan*, which together mean "person of the forest." Orangs are also sometimes referred to as "red apes" because of the long, russet-colored hair on their bodies.

There is only one species of orangutan, and it has the scientific name *Pongo pygmaeus*. It includes two subspecies, the orangutans from Borneo and those from Sumatra. They are similar in their habits and behavior, and when they are kept together in captivity, they can interbreed. Although the body hair of Bornean orangs is sometimes darker than that of the Sumatrans, the main difference between the two subspecies is in the appearance of the adult male. As a Bornean male matures, he develops huge cheek flaps and a pouch under his chin.

A Sumatran male is often taller and more slender than a Bornean male and usually does not have prominent cheek flaps or a pouch. Instead, his face is often adorned with a long mustache and beard. Both males have body hair that resembles a thick, unkempt rug. Except for Willie, all of the orangs at the Los Angeles Zoo are of the type found in Borneo. The appearance of individuals varies widely, and the only accurate way to determine if an animal is Bornean or Sumatran is by analyzing its body chemistry.

Louis, a male Bornean orangutan.

Adult male orangutans are usually about 4½ feet (1.4 meters) tall, although they sometimes grow to be more than 5 feet (1.5 meters). In captivity they may weigh as much as 350 pounds (159.1 kilograms); but in the wild, where food is less plentiful and the animals are more active, males usually weigh 130 to 200 pounds (59.1 to 90.9 kilograms). Because of their weight, full-grown males cannot climb as easily as younger animals, and they tend to spend more time on the ground. Cheek flaps begin to develop when a male is five or six, but they do not become fully developed until a male reaches his full growth, when he is about fifteen.

Female orangutans are only about half as big as males and usually weigh about 88 to 110 pounds (40 to 50 kilograms) and stand about 45 inches (1.1 meters) tall. Their body hair is not as thick as that on males, and females have narrow faces—more like those of younger animals.

Like other apes, young orangs grow up slowly, not reaching their full size until they are in their early teens. A male orangutan can mate when he is ten or eleven, and a female is able to have her first baby when she is eight or nine years old.

Male orangutan.   *Female orangutan.*

After a successful mating, the female is pregnant for about nine months before giving birth, usually to a single infant, although sometimes twins or triplets are born.

A newborn orang has fine hair on its back, head, and limbs, and weighs about 3 pounds (1.4 kilograms). Although it instinctively knows how to grasp its mother's hair, it is otherwise completely helpless. At first the baby clings to its mother's belly as she moves around. Later, as the baby grows stronger, it learns to ride on its mother's back. Like human babies, young orangs grow quickly in their first years. By his second birthday Michael will weigh about 18 pounds (8.2 kilograms).

Usually a mother animal knows how to take care of her baby instinctively. Sometimes, however, a new mother does not seem to be able to care for her infant. This is what happened when Michael was born. His mother, Eloise, ignored him, as she had her two earlier offspring. Those babies, Pumpkin and Rosie, had been raised in the zoo nursery and returned to the orangutan group when they could take care of themselves. However, when Michael was born, the keepers decided to see if one of the other orangutan females would act as a foster mother to him. They offered Michael to Sally, whose last-born youngster no longer needed her. Sally, who is actually Michael's grandmother, immediately took over his care and since then has raised him as her own.

During his first year, Michael never left Sally's side, but as he grew older and stronger he began to explore on his own. Like other youngsters, Michael is curious about everything in the world around him. Whenever he finds something new, he picks it up, feels it, and often tastes it to see if it might be good to eat.

One of Michael's favorite activities is climbing on the ropes in the enclosure. Using both his hands and feet to hold on, he climbs and swings much as a child would play on a jungle gym.

Although it looks as if a young orang climbs just for fun, this kind of activity helps its muscles grow strong and develops coordination and climbing skills.

As Michael grows older, he will learn to swing from rope to rope like the other orangs. In the wild, a mother orang must teach her baby to swing through the trees. An orangutan's arms, which stretch up to 8 feet (2.4 meters) from fingertip to fingertip, are one-and-a-half times as long as its legs and can swing in all directions. By grasping a branch or a vine with one hand, then swinging the body forward so that the other hand can catch another branch, an orangutan can move quickly through the treetops, often much faster than a person can move over the same distance on the ground. This kind of movement is called brachiation. Although orangs are skilled acrobats, they do sometimes fall.

Although wild orangs live mostly in the trees, they occasionally come down to the ground. Like other apes, orangs cannot walk completely upright. They can stand and walk for short distances on two legs, but they usually move on the ground with four limbs. An orang walks on the side of its foot rather than on the sole.

Orangutans are mainly vegetarians, and in the wild they spend most of each day moving through the forest in search of trees with ripe fruit. They are known to eat over three hundred kinds of foods, including fruits, vegetables, leaves, shoots, flowers, bark, insects, and eggs. At the zoo the animals are fed a variety of the fruits and vegetables in season. Their diet also includes pellets of monkey chow, eggs, milk, and a daily vitamin pill. The menu varies from day to day to provide a balance of nutrients as well as to keep their meals from becoming boring.

Although most of the orangutans' food is given to them in their night-time enclosure, the keepers also put out different kinds of foods and plants in the exhibit area each morning. The keepers often leave the plants unprepared so that the orangs can break them up and extract the edible parts just as they would in the wild.

Orangutans have large, strong jaws and, like people, they have thirty-two teeth. Sharp teeth in the front of the mouth can be used to pierce tough fruit rinds or to scrape off the soft insides of stems or bark. Sturdy molars in the back of the mouth are good for chewing or cracking nuts. The canine teeth of adult males are enlarged and are used for self-defense and in fighting with each other.

Michael began to nibble on pieces of fruits and vegetables when he was a few months old, but like other baby mammals, his first food was milk. Because Sally had been producing milk for her earlier offspring, Michael was able to drink her milk just as he would have from his own mother. A female orangutan gives her youngster milk until it is four or five years old. At that age, adolescent orangutans usually leave their mothers and form small groups until they are ready to mate and go off on their own.

Unlike gorillas and chimpanzees, which usually live in groups, wild orangutans most often live alone or with just a few other animals. Food in the rain forest is scattered over a wide area, and the orangs must be on the move constantly to satisfy their large appetites. If they lived in large groups, it would be difficult to find enough food in one place to feed everyone. In the zoo, where food is plentiful, the orangs are accustomed to living close together and get along well with each other.

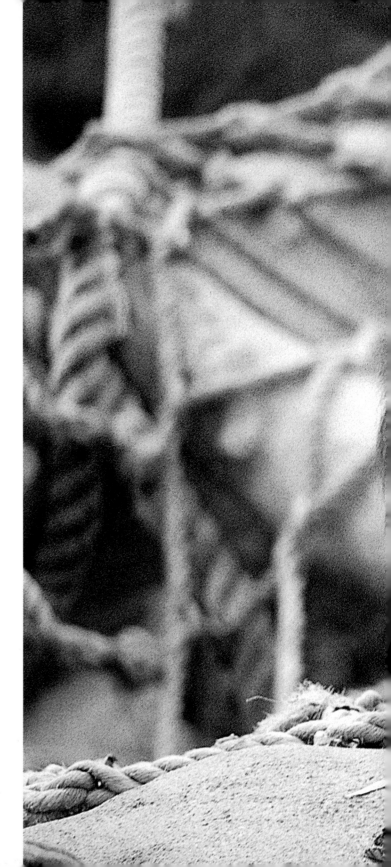

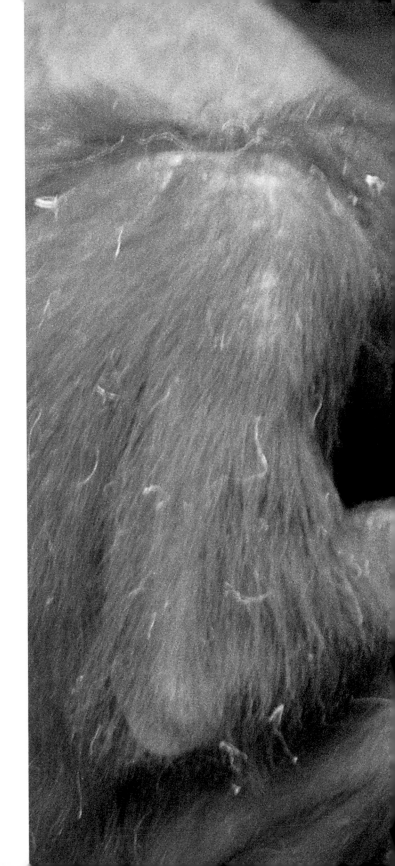

One of the ways that orangutans interact with each other is to pick through each other's hair, looking for dirt, insects, or tangles. This activity is called grooming. Mother orangs groom their babies, and older orangs that are living together sometimes groom each other.

34

Adult female orangutans usually live alone or with their young offspring. Sometimes two females and their young may come together for a few days, but they do not stay together permanently.

Because orangs are usually solitary, young orangs in the wild rarely have the chance to play with others their own age. However, at the zoo, Michael has three-and-a-half-year-old Pumpkin for a playmate. One of their favorite games is to chase each other and tumble on the ground together. Because he is older, Pumpkin is stronger. If the play becomes too rough, Michael squeals to let Pumpkin know he has had enough.

Adult male orangutans almost always live alone. In the wild, each adult male usually controls the part of the forest in which he lives. He declares his presence by emitting a loud, piercing call that tells other males to stay away. By inflating the pouch under his chin, a male can deepen his call and turn it into a loud roar. Male orangutans sometimes fight, usually over the right to mate with females, and older animals often have battle scars.

A female orangutan usually mates with the strongest male in her part of the forest. The male's loud call lets females that are ready to mate know where he is. During the period of mating, which may last for a week or so, a male and female orangutan stay together, eating and sleeping in the same area. After that, the female leaves and the male takes no more interest in her.

At the zoo, Louis, who is the father of Michael and Pumpkin, is the largest and strongest male in the group. He spends much of his time sitting alone on the highest rock overlooking the enclosure. Although eight-year-old Louie will not be fully grown for several more years, he is beginning to challenge Louis's position as the top male in the group. Frequently he punches him, teases him, or tries to take away some of his food. Louis responds by pushing back or threatening to attack.

Usually Louis wins these encounters because he is so much bigger and stronger, but Louie, who is quicker, can sometimes outmaneuver him. Eventually Louie will take over Louis's position.

Like other primates, orangutans communicate with each other by means of sounds. A grunt or bark may be used as a warning; a soft hoot may indicate distress; and when playing or being tickled, orangutans make sounds that are similar to laughter.

Facial expressions and gestures are another important way of communicating for orangs. A fixed stare or an open mouth with bared teeth indicates a threat. When the mouth is open and the teeth are covered, it means that the orang wants to play. Lips pursed in the form of a kiss show that the orang is begging for food.

Orangutans do not have vocal cords like those of humans and cannot make the kinds of sounds needed for human speech. Yet some have been taught to communicate with people in sign language or with symbols.

Although orangutans and other apes can learn words, they do not seem to be able to use them to form complex sentences or to express more than simple thoughts. An ape can ask for food, a toy, or a hug, but cannot discuss philosophy. The ability to use language in creative, complex ways is a uniquely human characteristic.

Scientists who study apes are very careful to avoid giving them human characteristics. Yet as we have learned more about apes, we see that they are like us in more ways than we previously thought. Groups of chimpanzees have been seen making warlike raids on their neighbors. Other apes have been observed playing tricks on each other. Observations of apes also show that they seem to experience many of the same emotions that we do, including fear, anger, contentment, and even jealousy. Despite the similarities, it is clear that we are very different from our apelike ancestors.

One of the striking aspects of orangutans is their intelligence—they are considered by many to be the most intelligent of all land animals. Young orangs are sometimes trained to act in circuses or in movies. They are good imitators and can use tools.

One of the differences between wild and captive orangs is that wild orangs almost never use objects as tools, whereas orangs in captivity learn quickly to manipulate whatever they find. Orangs are curious about their environment, and they quickly investigate and experiment with anything new in their enclosure. The orangutans at the zoo seem to use everything in their enclosure as tools or toys. A stiff cornstalk, for instance, can become a stick for digging or poking into a hollow log to search for seeds or nuts the keeper sometimes hides inside. The orangs use short reeds as drinking straws and long reeds looped over branches to swing from. A hollow pumpkin is both food and a drinking cup, and a rubber tub can become a nest or a portable roof.

After a morning of eating and playing, Michael is ready for an afternoon nap. Usually he sleeps in Sally's lap or cuddled up next to her. Most of the orangs relax during the middle of the day, especially when the weather is hot. Then toward the end of the afternoon, as the temperature grows cooler, they become more active before it is time to go inside. In the zoo, the orangs rest either on ledges on the rocks or, at night, on elevated platforms inside their enclosure.

Wild orangs sleep on platforms of leaves and branches which they build high in the trees. To make the nest, the orang bends several branches together, weaving or twisting them to make a flat, springy bed. Because the orangs are constantly moving through the forest in search of food, a new sleeping nest is constructed every day, and rarely used a second time. Roofs of leaves are often put over the nests to provide protection from the wind and rain.

Wild orangutans have few natural predators, and as long as they stay in the trees, they are safe from most dangers except for falling. Their main enemies are people and, on the island of Sumatra, tigers that roam the forest floor.

Orangutans usually live to be about forty years old and, in zoos, sometimes even longer than that. The oldest orang at the Los Angeles Zoo is Sally, who is thirty-six. One problem for orangs is that even though they live a long time, they reproduce slowly. A female orangutan may only have three or four youngsters in her lifetime, and not all of them may survive. Thus the population cannot increase quickly if a large number of animals are killed or die. Although there have been laws prohibiting the hunting or capture of orangutans for many years, some are still killed illegally by hunters.

The survival of orangutans depends both on protecting them in the wild and taking good care of them in captivity. With comfortable quarters, plenty of food, and good medical care, the number of captive orangutans has been growing. Many zoos have been successful in breeding orangutans, and they often share animals.

A program called the Species Survival Plan (SSP) keeps track of all orangutans in captivity and makes sure that animals which are closely related do not breed with each other. This helps to ensure stronger, healthier animals that will have a greater chance of surviving and producing their own young. Because Michael is closely related to most of the other orangutans at the Los Angeles Zoo, he will probably be sent elsewhere when he grows up so that he can mate with other females. Species Survival Plans exist for other endangered animals as well.

The future for orangutans is with young animals like Michael. As he grows up, he will help us learn more about the magnificent red ape. Orangutans are one of the links to our past. Without them, we would lose a valuable part of our own history.

INDEX

Photographs are in **boldface**.